A Gift of

The Wellesley
Free Library
Centennial Fund

A Taste of Culture

Foods of Vietnam

Barbara Sheen

KIDHAVEN PRESS

An imprint of Thomson Gale, a part of The Thomson Corporation

THOMSON

GALE

Detroit • New York • San Francisco • San Diego • New Haven, Conn. • Waterville, Maine • London • Munich

© 2006 by KidHaven Press. KidHaven Press is an imprint of The Gale Group, Inc., a division of Thomson Learning, Inc.

KidHaven™ and Thomson Learning™ are trademarks used herein under license.

For more information, contact
KidHaven Press
27500 Drake Rd.
Farmington Hills, MI 48331-3535
Or you can visit our Internet site at http://www.gale.com

LIBRARY OF CONGRESS CATALOGING-IN-PUBLICATION DATA
Sheen, Barbara.
Foods of Vietnam / by Barbara Sheen.
p. cm. — (A taste of culture)
Includes bibliographical references and index.
ISBN 0-7377-3452-3 (hard cover : alk. paper) 1. Cookery, Vietnamese.
2. Vietnam—Social life and customs. I. Title. II. Series.
TX724.5.V5S54 2006
641.59597—dc22
2005018664

Printed in the United States of America

Contents

Chapter 1

Unique Ingredients

Vietnamese food is delicious, colorful, and fragrant. It uses fresh ingredients that delight the senses. Rice, fish sauce, and freshly picked herbs give Vietnamese cuisine its distinctive character and flavor. Vietnamese cooks use these ingredients in most every dish they make.

The Pearl of the Gods

The Vietnamese call rice "The Pearl of the Gods." Rice is the basis of every Vietnamese meal and an important part of Vietnamese life. Lush, green rice paddies snake across Vietnam. The majority of the Vietnamese people make their living growing or selling rice, and have been doing so since 3000 B.C.

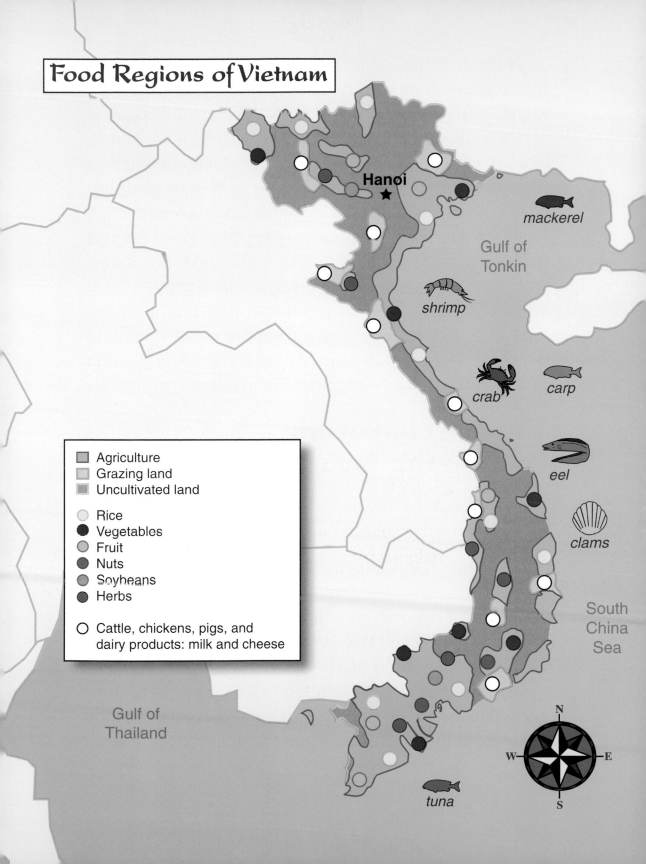

The Vietnamese grow dozens of different varieties of rice, each with its own distinctive flavor and fragrance. Many Vietnamese people say that they can tell what kind of rice is cooking simply by the aroma. There is white rice, black rice, sticky short grain rice, and sweet-smelling jasmine rice, just to name a few. Each is used in its own special way. For instance, sticky white rice, also known as sweet glutinous rice, is often mixed with vegetables and meat, wrapped in a banana leaf, and boiled. Black rice, with its nutty flavor, is eaten as a snack topped with crushed peanuts and shredded coconut. Fluffy, tender long grain rice is the most commonly eaten mealtime rice. The most popular form of long grain rice is jasmine rice. Its sweet, flowery fragrance is considered irresistible.

The Most Important Food on the Table

Rice or rice products are a part of every Vietnamese meal. In fact, a bowl of jasmine rice and a dash of fish sauce is considered a meal in itself. For some people, even the most elaborate meal is considered incomplete without rice. A typical family meal consists of individual bowls of rice served with meat or seafood, dipping sauce, and a salad. However, it is the rice that is the most important food on the table.

Not just any rice will do. The Vietnamese are quite particular about the way rice is prepared. It must be perfectly cooked until it is piping hot and fluffy. Chef Diana My Tran, who was born and raised in Vietnam, describes

A Vietnamese farmer poses with her basket before harvesting rice from a paddy. Rice is the heart and soul of Vietnamese food.

the typical Vietnamese attitude towards cooking rice: "[We] would rather have perfectly cooked rice and a plain bowl of fish sauce than badly cooked rice with any number of delicious entrees."[1] To accomplish this, Vietnamese cooks rinse uncooked rice repeatedly while swirling it around between their fingers. This cleans the rice and removes excess starch. Removing some of the starch keeps the rice from becoming too sticky.

Vietnamese farm workers enjoy a hearty outdoor meal of jasmine rice and a fish stew.

A Versatile Staple

The Vietnamese have many other uses for rice. They grind rice into flour, which is turned into noodles, crunchy rolls called **baguettes** (*baa-getz*), and delicate **rice paper**.

When a bowl of rice is not served, rice noodles are. Rice paper, on the other hand, is often served with rice. Like its name, rice paper is as thin as paper and pearly white. It tastes bland and is soft and chewy. Little squares of rice paper are usually served with every meal. The Vietnamese wrap tidbits of food inside the opaque paper and dip the wrap in fish sauce.

Fish and Seafood

Fish is almost as important an ingredient as rice. Vietnam has 1,864 miles (3,000km) of coastline, as well as many inland waterways where fish and seafood are plentiful. Bustling fish markets are found all over Vietnam,

A street vendor in southern Vietnam demonstrates her skill at making rice paper. These thin, chewy squares are served with most meals.

in which dozens of different kinds of fish and seafood are sold. Tuna, mackerel, carp, eel, crabs, clams, and shrimp are all part of the Vietnamese diet. The Vietnamese fry them or steam them, and serve them with rice, herbs, and dipping sauce. Fish are cooked whole, and shellfish are cooked in their shells. This keeps them moist, sweet, and tender.

The Flavor of Vietnam

Fish is also the basis for **nuoc mam** (*nuke mom*), a unique sauce that is often called the flavor of Vietnam. It is so much a part of Vietnamese cooking that many Vietnamese people say food does not taste good without it.

Nuoc mam is a liquid that is drained from salted, fermented, anchovy-like fish. It has a salty, tangy flavor and aroma. Phan, a Vietnamese man, explains: "A good

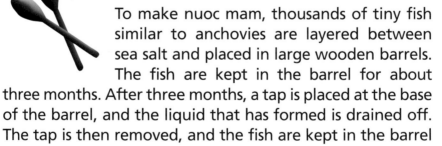

Making Nuoc Mam

To make nuoc mam, thousands of tiny fish similar to anchovies are layered between sea salt and placed in large wooden barrels. The fish are kept in the barrel for about three months. After three months, a tap is placed at the base of the barrel, and the liquid that has formed is drained off. The tap is then removed, and the fish are kept in the barrel for another three months, at which time the barrel is tapped again. This procedure often goes on for years.

The finest nuoc mam comes from the first draining. Nuoc mam from the first draining is used to make dipping sauce, while nuoc mam from later drainings is used in cooking.

Vietnamese Rice

The Vietnamese are particular about their rice, and prepare it very carefully. This recipe calls for long-grain jasmine rice. It is quite fragrant, but any long-grain rice can be used.

Ingredients

2 cups long-grain jasmine rice
water

Instructions

1. Put the rice in a pot. Pour 2 cups of water over the rice. With clean hands, run your fingers through the rice. The water will turn white with starch that comes off the rice.
2. Drain the water from the pot, and repeat step 1 again. Drain again.
3. Add $2^1/2$ cups of clean water to the rice. Cover the pot and bring the water to a boil.
4. Lower the heat to medium and cook the rice until all the water is absorbed. This should take around 20 minutes.
5. When the water is absorbed, turn off the heat and let the rice sit in the covered pot for 5 minutes.
6. Use a fork or spoon to gently fluff the rice before serving.

Serves 4–6

Workers in a busy Vietnamese fish market sort through baskets of small fish for sale.

nuoc mam should smell like the ocean on a sunny day, pleasant and aromatically salty."[2]

The Vietnamese use nuoc mam to season seafood, fish, meat, vegetables, and soup. Its salty flavor blends well with other foods during cooking. However, nuoc mam is too salty to be eaten by itself as a dipping sauce. That is why the Vietnamese invented **nuoc cham** (*nuke cam*).

Nuoc Cham

Nuoc cham is nuoc mam to which hot peppers, garlic, sugar, water, and lime juice are added. It tastes salty, spicy, sweet, and tart all at the same time. Most Vietnamese cooks have their own recipes, adding ingredients like carrots, ginger, or **coconut milk** to the sauce to give it a distinct flavor. The Vietnamese drizzle nuoc cham on rice and noodles. They also dip vegetables, meat, and fish into the sauce. Like salt and pepper in the West, nuoc cham is found on every Vietnamese table. "A meal without nuoc cham is no meal at all,"[3] says chef Corinne Trang, who was raised in Vietnam.

Fragrant Herbs

Vietnam has long been known for its herbs and spices. Roman traders seeking herbs and spices journeyed to Vietnam as early as A.D. 166. Sixteenth-century Portuguese explorers came to Vietnam with the same goal.

Table Salad

This table salad can be eaten like a traditional salad, or the leaves can be used as wrappers for meat or fish.

Ingredients

1 bunch Asian basil
1 bunch mint
1 bunch cilantro
5 ounces baby spinach
1/2 cucumber, peeled and thinly sliced

Instructions

1. Wash and dry the greens.
2. Arrange the greens and cucumber slices in separate groups on a large plate.

Serves 6–8.

By the 19th century, Vietnam was known to most of the world as "The Land of Spices."

Dozens of different varieties of herbs grow wild there. They thrive along the banks of rivers and rice fields. Among the favorites are licorice-scented Asian basil, red perilla (a purple stemmed plant with fuzzy leaves and a lemony taste), fresh-flavored spearmint, and spicy **cilantro**.

A Vietnamese farm worker rows a boat filled with fresh vegetables and herbs to a market along the Mekong River.

Fresh herbs add color, flavor, and aroma to Vietnamese food. The Vietnamese use fresh herbs to flavor soups. They pound herbs, like citrusy **lemongrass**, into a paste to use as a sweet-smelling rub for grilled meat and as a flavoring for dipping sauces.

More importantly, the Vietnamese eat herbs with every meal in the form of a table salad. This large platter overflows with piles of rau thom (*row thum*), or fresh, aromatic herbs. Sprigs of different types of mints, basils, and lettuce all are likely to be part of the salad. The selection varies according to the accompanying dishes so that the flavors complement each other. For example, a table salad of different types of mint and red and green perilla can accompany grilled meat, while Asian basil and savory saw-leaf are served with noodles. Vietnamese diners do not eat the salad the way Westerners do. Instead of piling it on their plate, they tear off bits of the fragrant greens, which they add to their cooked food or use to wrap around bits of meat or seafood and dip into nuoc cham. According to chef Mai Pham, who was born and raised in Vietnam, "A single diner can easily consume two or three bunches of fresh herbs, picking the leaves off the sprigs as the meal progresses."[4] The contrast of hot tender meat and seafood and cool crunchy herbs is delicious and uniquely Vietnamese.

Fresh herbs, jasmine-scented rice, and salty, savory fish sauce give Vietnamese cooking its distinctive taste, color, and fragrance. These unique ingredients are the flavors of Vietnam.

A Delicious Mix

Vietnamese cooking has been influenced by China and France, two nations that once ruled Vietnam. They brought cooking methods such as stir-frying, and foods like noodles, soy sauce, beef, and baguettes to Vietnam. Creative Vietnamese cooks took the best from these two diverse cooking styles and added their own favorite ingredients. The result is distinctly Vietnamese. Three favorite dishes—**pho** (*fo*), **claypot** stews, and singing **crepes** (*creps*)—characterize this delicious mix.

Pho, the National Dish of Vietnam

Pho is one of the most popular dishes in Vietnam. This clear, fragrant broth is filled with rice noodles and meats such as beef sirloin, meatballs, chicken, or pork,

A young man at an outdoor café enjoys a steaming pot of pho, the national dish of Vietnam.

A girl wearing traditional Vietnamese dress uses chopsticks to eat the noodles from a bowl of pho.

and topped with ginger, fresh herbs, and vegetables. "We could eat it morning and night, day after day,"[5] explains Vietnamese writer Duong Thu Huong.

The Vietnamese have been eating pho for about 100 years. It is a clever mix of Vietnamese spices, Chinese noodles, and the French method of using beef bones to make broth. To make pho, cooks simmer beef bones in water flavored with nuoc mam, sugar, ginger, cinnamon, and star anise, a spice that looks like a little star and tastes like licorice. The aroma of the spices simmering in the fresh broth can be almost as irresistible as the beefy, savory-sweet flavor. "When my husband and I were first married, we would stop by a pho restaurant for breakfast

Easy Pho with Chicken

Pho is made from fresh beef stock that takes hours to make. This recipe uses canned beef broth to make cooking faster and easier.

Ingredients

3 cans beef consommé
1/2 pound cooked chicken, cut into thin small pieces
4 ounces rice noodles
1 teaspoon ground ginger
1 cinnamon stick
1 small onion, peeled and cut in quarters
1 cup bean sprouts
4 slices of lime
4 green onions, sliced
1 jalapeno pepper, seeded and minced
1/4 pound fresh basil

before going to work. I shall never forget the aroma coming from the huge soup pot,"[6] recalls Tran.

It can take up to 24 hours for the broth to cook. The longer it simmers, the richer, tastier, and more nourishing it becomes. When the broth is almost done, the cook soaks the noodles in cold water for 30 minutes. This makes them so tender that they only need to cook for 20 seconds. The cooked noodles are soft and chewy, just the way the Vietnamese like them.

When the noodles are done, the cook slides them into large, preheated bowls. Next, diners choose which

Instructions

1. Cook the noodles according to the package directions.
2. Put the consommé, ginger, cinnamon stick, and onion in a pot and bring to a boil. Lower the heat and let the soup simmer for 15 minutes.
3. Divide the noodles among 4–6 bowls, depending on the number of people being served, and put the chicken slices on top of the noodles.
4. Strain the soup, and pour the strained soup over the noodles and chicken.
5. Put the lime slices, green onion, jalapeno slices, bean sprouts, and basil on separate plates. Serve with the soup.

Serves 4–6.

meat they want. If beef tenderloin is chosen, a few slices of raw beef are added. Because the beef is sliced paper-thin, when the hot broth is poured over it, the beef cooks instantly. Thicker cuts of meat and chicken are already cooked.

Pho is always served with a choice of **garnishes**, like chili sauce, cilantro, bean sprouts, lime wedges, and onions. Diners choose their favorites, adding as much or as little as they like. Then, holding chopsticks in one

Eating Pho

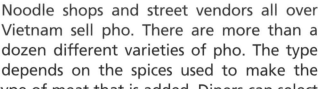

Noodle shops and street vendors all over Vietnam sell pho. There are more than a dozen different varieties of pho. The type depends on the spices used to make the broth and the type of meat that is added. Diners can select bits of brisket, meatballs, almost translucent slices of tenderloin, tripe or intestines, or chicken.

Pho is served in different size bowls. The smallest bowl amply feeds one person, and the largest, which is called "train-size," can easily feed three hungry individuals.

No matter the bowl size, diners want their pho to be red-hot. If the broth cools down, the noodles expand and become sticky. That is why the Vietnamese often wait to visit and talk until they have finished eating. But even though diners may not be talking, it is still noisy. That is because, in Vietnam, it is polite to loudly slurp your pho.

A young boy slurps up noodles from a bowl of piping hot pho.

hand and a spoon in the other, diners vary between pulling out the noodles and spooning up the broth. The Vietnamese consider a bowl of pho a complete meal. It is, according to Vietnamese food expert Richard Sterling, Vietnamese "soul food."[7]

Bean Sprouts

One-of-a-Kind Stews

Stews, cooked Vietnamese-style, are another way the Vietnamese have adapted French and Chinese cooking. Most Vietnamese stews are cooked in claypots, which were brought to Vietnam by the ancient Chinese and are quite similar to earthenware pots used by the French to make stews. Made of sand and clay, they resemble flowerpots with lids. They are pretty to look at, and they cook food perfectly.

Heat is evenly distributed in claypots. As the pot heats up, it releases water droplets that lightly moisten and steam the food inside. This keeps the ingredients from drying out and having a tough texture. Instead, they become tender with smoky flavor that comes from the mixture of the clay and wood, charcoal, or gas fire over which the stew is cooked. When the claypot's cover is removed, the scent is fantastic.

The Vietnamese make dozens of different types of claypot stews. Every family has their own special recipes. Claypot stew is a very common Vietnamese dish during winter. The stews are as popular for breakfast as they are for lunch and dinner. Claypot stews are,

Clay pots filled with delicious pork stew (left) cook over an open fire (above).

according to Pham, "The one dish that best represents Vietnamese home cooking. . . . It's a favorite at every family table."[8]

A Blend of Flavors

Most claypot stews are simmered slowly, so that all the flavors can blend together. Many claypot dishes like bo kho (*ball call*), or beef stew, are sweet and spicy. Bo kho combines carrots, nuoc mam, beef, onions, garlic, star anise, chilies, cinnamon, and coconut juice, among other ingredients. Claypot chicken has a zesty flavor that comes from a combination of lime juice, nuoc mam, lemongrass, and soy sauce mixed with chicken, onions, mushrooms, and bok choy, a type of cabbage.

Thit kho tieu (*tit call chu*), or claypot pork, is another favorite. To make this popular dish, thin, bite-sized slices of pork are marinated in a sauce made with nuoc mam and nuoc mau, a sweet Vietnamese caramel sauce. The

The Vietnamese Kitchen

Kitchens in Vietnam are different from kitchens in North America. Country kitchens are often outdoor rooms without walls, covered by a thatch roof. Few have a refrigerator. In order to keep food fresh, most Vietnamese cooks shop at least once a day.

At the center of most Vietnamese kitchens is a charcoal or wood-burning stove. These stoves are low to the ground. Most Vietnamese cooks squat on the floor while cooking with their pots and cooking utensils beside them.

Among these pots and utensils are a bamboo steamer for cooking rice, and a wok, which is a round, Chinese frying pan that is used for stir-frying. There is always a razor-sharp meat cleaver that is used to cut food into bite-sized pieces before it is cooked. Knives are not placed on the table. There is also a pair of extra long chop sticks. These are used for stirring hot foods while they are cooking. Smaller chopsticks are used for eating.

pork and remaining marinade are put in a claypot with water, black pepper, green onions, and cilantro. As the stew cooks, the sauce forms a salty-sweet syrup that coats the meat.

Vietnamese cooks usually serve claypot pork over hot steamed rice with pickled bean sprouts on the side. Sometimes it is served with crusty bread made from rice flour or inside a hollowed-out roll.

Singing Crepes

Sizzling singing crepes are another way the Vietnamese have adapted French and Chinese recipes to create one of Vietnam's favorite dishes. Sizzling dishes are a Chinese creation, and crepes, which are delicately thin pancakes, are French. Unlike French crepes, which are made from wheat flour, Vietnamese crepes are made from rice flour. This gives them a more delicate texture than French crepes. Their flavor is also uniquely Vietnamese. This is because coconut milk, green onions, sugar, and turmeric, a spice, are added to the batter. They taste sweet, savory, crispy, chewy, and light, all at the same time. Author Andrea Q. Nguyen describes this unique Vietnamese creation as "crispy in texture and toasty in flavor, with an alluring chewiness, like that of perfectly cooked rice."[9]

To make singing crepes, the cook rapidly stir-fries bite-size pieces of shrimp, pork, bean sprouts, and mushrooms, although the exact ingredients can vary. To make sure everything cooks evenly, he or she continuously moves the ingredients around in the pot. Next, the cook pours the batter over the ingredients.

A Vietnamese street vendor gently swirls the stir-fried ingredients of a batch of singing crepes.

Singing Crepes

This is an easy way to make singing crepes. Coconut milk and rice flour are available in Asian grocery stores and many supermarkets.

Ingredients

2 cups rice flour
1 teaspoon sugar
$1/2$ cup coconut milk
$2 1/3$ cups water
$1/2$ teaspoon turmeric
$1/2$ teaspoon salt
1 green onion, chopped
$1/2$ tablespoon vegetable oil
$1/3$ lb. cooked shrimp, peeled, deveined, tails removed, and cut into bite-sized pieces
1 carrot, peeled and shredded
1 cup bean sprouts

Instructions

1. Mix the carrot and shrimp together and set aside.
2. Mix together the flour and all the other ingredients, except the bean sprouts.

When the batter hits the hot pot, it makes a "see-see-see" sizzling sound almost as if the crepes are singing, which is how they got their name.

To keep the batter from pooling, the cook swirls the pan around. When the sides and bottom of the crepe form a crunchy crust and the top is soft, chewy, and golden, the crepe is folded over like an omelet and slid out of the pan onto a sheet of rice paper. The cook nimbly wraps the rice paper around the crepe and places it

3. Heat the oil in a frying pan. When the oil is hot, pour ¼ of the flour mixture into the frying pan. Shake the pan to distribute the batter evenly and fry the crepe for 3 minutes.
4. Remove the crepe. Spread ¼ of the shrimp mixture on one side of the crepe, and top with ¼ of the bean sprouts. Fold the crepe over the filling.
5. To make four crepes, repeat the cooking process three more times.

Serve the crepes with lettuce leaves, fresh herbs, and nuoc cham.

Serves 4.

on a large platter. Diners tear off pieces of the crunchy package and wrap it in mustard greens or fresh herbs that they pull from the table salad. They then dip it into nuoc cham.

It is not surprising that these musical crepes are also known as "happy crepes." Their crisp, chewy texture, blend of flavors, and song can bring a smile to a diner's face, as can the distinct taste of claypot stews, and rich, beefy pho. No wonder these dishes are favorites in Vietnam.

A Snack on Every Corner

Snacks are popular in Vietnam. Streets are crowded with cafés and small stalls offering dozens of treats. Enticed by the aromas, hungry passersby stand at counters or sit on little stools and lawn chairs savoring one delicacy after another. Among the favorites are leaf-wrapped cakes, Vietnamese sandwiches, and sweet tropical puddings.

All Wrapped Up

Banh (*bun*) is the Vietnamese word for cake. These sweet and savory treats are nothing like the dessert pastry known as cake in the West. To the Vietnamese, any small, portable food that can be eaten without chopsticks is called cake. This includes sandwiches,

A vendor heaps layers of different foods in large banana leaves to prepare the tasty snack known as banh.

A man smoothes out enormous banana leaves that he will use to wrap up banh.

baked goods, spring rolls, and what might be the most popular banh of all—leaf wraps. These tiny treats, which are securely wrapped in banana leaves, tied with lots of tight little knots, and grilled over an open fire, are the Vietnamese answer to fast food. In fact, banh gio, a combination of rice dough and minced pork, is the same size and shape as a hamburger.

Cooking food in leaves is one of the oldest and most clever forms of cooking. The Vietnamese have been doing it for centuries. The leaves serve as both a cooking pot and a plate. The broad center rib of the leaf, which is removed before banh is cooked, can be used as a spoon. The leaves also keep the food inside from getting

Shopping in Vietnam

Besides having modern supermarkets and convenience stores, Vietnam has many tradi-tional markets. These are like miniature vil-lages where shoppers can find a remarkable array of fresh, raw products and cooked snacks. There are also floating markets that are held entirely on water. Here small boats filled with different fresh specialties converge in the center of rivers, where shoppers in other boats make their pur-chases. Because there are so many boats, shoppers can ac-tually hop out of their own boat and walk from boat to boat without getting wet.

Shoppers looking for specialty foods make their way from boat to boat in a floating market in southern Vietnam.

dirty or spoiling. Plus when they are grilled, the leaves give off a licorice-like flavor and fragrance that filters through to the food inside. Because of their portability and good taste, ancient Vietnamese farmers, fishers, and soldiers depended on them.

Round, square, tubular, or triangular, these little packages are sold all over Vietnam. According to Sterling, "They fill baskets with their abundance, sit neatly stacked on countertops, and hang in clusters from eaves, crossbeams, or stall corners—edible ornaments."[10]

Not only are they pretty, but they are filled with so many different delicacies that there is something for everyone. Some contain only one treat—a piece of spicy pork, or a bit of yam. Others offer layer after layer of surprises—a ball of sticky rice stuffed with gingered shrimp and pork, or a see-through piece of rice paper filled with shredded coconut and beans. Though it takes patience to open them up, the taste of the treat inside makes it worth the effort for many people.

A Burst of Flavor

Sandwiches are another popular Vietnamese snack. Every village has at least one sandwich stand, and bigger towns and cities have dozens. Banh mi (*bun me*), a uniquely Vietnamese sandwich, is a top choice everywhere.

It all starts with a baguette, a long thin French roll, which the Vietnamese have transformed by mixing rice and wheat flour for the dough. The result is a light and airy roll with a crispy crust. It is a perfect match for the delicate ingredients that fill it.

A sandwich vendor spreads pâté on a baguette and heaps vegetables and herbs on the bread to make the perfect sandwich.

To make the sandwich, the cook starts by toasting the baguette on a grill. When the roll is hot and crunchy, it is sliced and the filling is added.

A layer of pork **pâté** (*pa-tay*) is spread on the roll. Pâté is another French creation. But French pâté tastes nothing like the Vietnamese meat spread, which is made from minced pork, garlic, sugar, nuoc mam, and dried chilies that have been finely ground and mixed together to form a spicy, spreadable treat. It is topped with slices of sweet, crisp barbequed pork, and salty Vietnamese pork sausage. The warm meats are garnished with cold vegetables and

Vietnamese Sandwich

This sandwich is not hard to make. It calls for ground pork, but ground beef or turkey can also be used. Bologna can be substituted for ham. Garnishes vary with individual taste. Feel free to be creative.

Ingredients

4 baguettes or other hard rolls, 6 inches long each
1/3 lb ground pork
1 teaspoon garlic powder
1/2 teaspoon crushed red pepper flakes
1 teaspoon sugar
2 teaspoons nuoc mam or other Asian fish sauce
2 tablespoons vegetable oil
4 slices of ham

Garnishes (optional)

1 jalapeno pepper, sliced
1 cucumber, cut into thin rings
various pickled vegetables
4 sprigs cilantro and spearmint
lime

Instructions

1. Mix together the sugar, pepper, garlic, and nuoc mam. Add it to the ground meat.
2. Heat the oil in a frying pan. When the oil is hot, add the meat mixture. Cook until the meat is brown, about 4 minutes. Remove the meat from the pan and set aside.
3. Cut the baguettes in half vertically. Toast in a toaster oven or over a grill.
4. Spread the ground pork mixture on 4 slices of the baguette, putting 1/4 of the mixture on each. Top with ham.
5. Add garnishes according to personal taste. If the lime is used, only the juice is squeezed onto the sandwich. Top with remaining baguette slices.

Serves 4.

crisp fresh herbs. These include icy pickled carrots, cucumbers, chilies, and radishes, as well as bunches of fresh cilantro and mint. The mix of contrasting tastes, textures, and temperatures is a true explosion of flavors. The sandwich is soft and crunchy, hot and cold, sweet, spicy, and salty, all at the same time. Each contrasting element complements the next. For many the taste is divine. Pham agrees, "One bite," she explains, "and I'm in heaven."[11]

Sweet Pudding

Che is another heavenly treat. This creamy pudding satisfies most everyone's sweet tooth.

The Vietnamese love sweets. However, they rarely eat them with meals. Instead, sugary snacks are offered on the streets all day long. Che is a favorite.

Che originated in Hanoi (in northern Vietnam) and spread across the rest of the country. Shops, markets,

A vendor on a Hanoi street scoops out bowls of che, a popular treat throughout Vietnam.

and street vendors have big metal pots filled to the brim with different types of che. Somewhat thinner than soft ice cream, che is a thick liquid that can almost be sipped through a straw. But the Vietnamese usually eat it with a long spoon.

Banana Coconut Che

This recipe calls for tapioca pearls. They can be purchased in Asian grocery stores and health food stores. Many supermarkets carry them.

Ingredients

3 tablespoons tapioca pearls
3 cups water
3 tablespoons sugar
1/2 cup coconut milk
pinch of salt
1 lb bananas cut into thin, round slices

Instructions

1. Bring the water to a boil in a large pot. Add the tapioca pearls. Stir well to keep the pearls from sticking together. Cook until the mixture thickens, about 10 minutes.
2. Mix the coconut milk, sugar, and salt together.
3. Stir the coconut milk mixture into the tapioca pearls. Cook until the sugar dissolves. Add the banana slices and cook 3 minutes.

Let the pudding cool to room temperature. Serve in individual bowls or glasses. Top with crushed ice.

Serves 6.

The Noodle Knocker

In Vietnam, it is common to hear the sound of two bamboo sticks knocking against each other. This is the sound of the noodle knocker announcing his or her presence. Noodle knockers, who are often children, carry with them noodle soup, cold noodle dishes, or grilled meat and shrimp. When people hear the noodle knockers, who walk through neighborhood after neighborhood, they call them to their front door and place an order.

There are many varieties of che. Among other ingredients, most che contains soft red, white, or green mung beans, sticky rice, sugar, and coconut milk. Tapioca pearls, a sticky paste made from cassava (a tuber that is similar to a sweet potato), thicken the mix and give it an interesting creamy, chewy texture.

Served in a tall glass, che can be hot, lukewarm, or ice-cold. Cold che is a popular summer snack. A topping of crushed or shaved ice and cold, sweetened coconut juice can make it as refreshing as ice cream on a hot day.

Infinite Varieties

Che cooks add dozens of different ingredients to this basic mix. Dark green Ten Ingredient Che is one of the most popular varieties. Cherries, dried bananas and apples, coconut paste, shaved coconut, crushed peanuts, lotus seeds, and agar-agar, a gelatin made from seaweed, are among its many ingredients. To enhance the scent and flavor, crushed pandanus leaves are thrown into the mix. This Asian plant tastes and smells just like vanilla, and is especially flavorful when combined with coconut. Before it is served, it is topped with shaved ice and bathed in sweetened coconut milk.

Che is a popular after-school snack. Teenagers often meet friends at che shops. Children will stop at che stands on their way home from school. "You can always tell where the dessert vendors sit at the market near my

For people craving a sweet snack, a che vendor is a welcome site on streets in Vietnam.

grandmother's house. It is where the schoolchildren congregate, peering excitedly at the big pots of che,"[12] Pham explains.

Che vendors walk along residential streets, a yoke-like bamboo pole slung across their shoulders with a bucket full of che hanging from each end. Seeing the vendors, people call them to their homes and buy their favorites for late night snacks. Tran recalls that her family ate, "a bowl of coconut pudding in the late evening, when I should have been in bed. . . . Together we ate these delicious puddings while watching television, savoring every spoonful."[13]

Whether relaxing at home, returning from school, or heading out to meet friends, the Vietnamese people have much to savor. With perfectly wrapped banh hanging from vendors' stalls, baguettes roasting on hot coals, and big pots overflowing with sweet che, it is no wonder that snacks are so well liked.

Getting Together and Feasting

Holidays give the Vietnamese people the chance to gather and celebrate with loved ones. During many holiday celebrations, the Vietnamese feast on festive foods that often have special meaning.

Tet, the three-day Vietnamese New Year's celebration, is the most important and grandest event of the year. It is New Year's, a family reunion, and a giant birthday party all rolled into one. Every person in Vietnam marks their birthday during Tet, no matter what the actual date of his or her birth is. Businesses close so that families can get together and feast. In fact, eating is so much a part of Tet that the Vietnamese people do not say that they celebrate Tet. Instead, they say that they "eat Tet."

During Tet every meal is a banquet that honors the spirits of dead ancestors who, the Vietnamese believe, return to Earth for the holiday. Piling the table with food is a way to welcome them. Although not everyone serves exactly the same food, two dishes—chicken and **banh chung** (*bun chung*)—are likely to be found on every holiday table.

A Symbol of Abundance

Because they produce both meat and eggs, chickens are highly valued in Vietnam. Serving chicken during Tet is considered a sign of abundance, and a symbol of future prosperity. The fresher the chicken is, the better.

Markets all over Vietnam sell live chickens. Shoppers select a bird. The vendor slaughters it, then removes

Wearing traditional clothing and holding food offerings, these Vietnamese women are celebrating Tet, Vietnam's most important holiday.

the feathers. Trang explains: "They are selected live by the customer, then are killed on the spot, as the Vietnamese prefer their poultry fresh (and you cannot get fresher than that)."[14]

Delicious Dishes

Once a chicken is selected, boiling is the most popular way of preparing it. Although boiled chicken often tastes bland, this is not the case in Vietnam. That is because before cooking the chicken, the cook rubs it with ginger. Even more ginger and cilantro are added to the cooking water. The fragrance perfumes the kitchen, and infuses the chicken with an exotic aroma and flavor.

The Vietnamese do not cook chicken for as long as Westerners do. They say that chicken is done when the meat is white, but the bones are still pink. That way the meat is never overcooked. Instead it is tender and juicy. As long as the meat itself is not pink, and therefore undercooked, there is little danger of food poisoning, which can be spread by eating undercooked poultry.

Once the chicken is done, the cook removes it from the pot and cuts it into bite-sized pieces. These are served atop a bed of jasmine rice and garnished with chopped lemon leaves and slices of lemongrass. A table salad and various dipping sauces accompany the chicken. There is nuoc cham, creamy peanut sauce, zesty chili-ginger sauce, and refreshing lime sauce. Dipping the chicken in these different sauces changes the flavor, making it seem as if more than one chicken dish has been served.

A street vendor offers live chickens for sale. Fresh chickens are a must for the Tet feast.

Vietnamese Boiled Chicken

This Tet favorite is easy to make and tastes delicious. Serve it with rice and your favorite dipping sauce.

Ingredients

1 whole chicken
4 sprigs of cilantro
2 teaspoons ground ginger
1 stalk fresh ginger, peeled and sliced
water

Instructions

1. Wash and clean the chicken. Sprinkle ground ginger on the clean chicken.
2. Fill a large pot with water. Boil the water. Add the chicken, fresh ginger, and cilantro. Cover the pot. Cook the chicken over low heat until it is done—about 1$\frac{1}{2}$–2 hours.
3. Remove the chicken from the pot. When it is cool enough to handle, slice the chicken.

   Serve with dipping sauce and fresh herbs.

   Serves 4–6.

Earth Cakes

Another traditional food that is found on every Tet table is banh chung or Earth cakes. The Vietnamese have been eating them during Tet for hundreds of years. To many, Tet would not be Tet without them. Banh chung are leaf-wrapped rice cakes stuffed with pork, sweet bean paste, and nuoc mam. They are not like snacking banh in that they are steamed rather than grilled and take more than a day to prepare. Because they require so much time and effort, they are reserved for special occasions.

Banh chung are made with beans that are soaked in water for four hours to soften them, and sticky rice that is soaked for an entire day, which causes the rice to expand. After soaking, the rice and beans are steamed in separate pots. The beans are then

A woman prepares banh chung (right), as her husband pounds sweet beans into the paste she needs to make more of the Tet treat.

The Legend of Banh Chung

According to legend, the first banh chung was created 4,000 years ago, when a Vietnamese king decided that whichever of his many sons created the best dish for Tet would become the next king. Prince Lang Lieu, the kindest son, was visited by a genie. The genie told the prince to make a dish with rice, because rice was so important to the Vietnamese people. And, it should be square in shape, because the ancient Vietnamese people believed the Earth was square. To make it flavorful, the prince was told to add pork, nuoc mam, and beans, wrap the dish in banana leaves, and cook it all day.

The king loved the banh chung and shared it with the Vietnamese people. Of course, Prince Lang Lieu became the next king, And from that day on, banh chung has been served during Tet.

pounded into a thick paste. While this is going on, the pork is cut into little tidbits and marinated in nuoc mam. Then, it is stir-fried.

Finally, the ingredients are ready to be wrapped. First a layer of rice is placed in the center of two perpendicular banana leaves. The bean paste is placed on top, followed by the pork, another layer of beans, and finally more rice. The edges of the leaves are gathered up, and the banh chung is formed into approximately 5-inch (12.70cm) square parcels tied tightly with strings of bamboo.

But the cooking process is not over yet. The little packages are put in a steamer basket and submerged in a pot of boiling water where they remain for up to ten hours. The hot steam moistens the banana leaves, dyeing the rice green.

Green of the Earth

Banh chung are usually eaten with pickled vegetables. They are served both hot and cold. Every home has a tray piled with banh chung ready for visitors, who bring even more of the little cakes tied with bright red ribbons as New Year's gifts. To the Vietnamese, the green rice cake is symbolic of the rice fields that carpet their country and provide them with their livelihood. By sharing the cakes at Tet, the Vietnamese share an important part of their lives. Tran Lien Hoan of Vietnam explains: "The cakes are made of sticky rice because the people of Vietnam live on rice. They are filled with pork and mung beans because everything that God gave us is in the cake."[15]

A Time for Children

Tet usually occurs at the start of spring. By fall, the Vietnamese are ready for another big celebration. Known as the Mid-Autumn Festival, which the Vietnamese have been celebrating for many centuries. This holiday, which marks the end of the rice harvest, is held when the moon appears

Bamboo

Five Fruit Tray

On the last night of Tet, a tray known as the "tray of to-getherness" is always served. It contains five fruits. The number represents the number of fingers on a hand, each of which works hard all year. The fruits vary. Nuts or seeds can be substituted for one or two fruits.

Ingredients

2 bananas, peeled and sliced into circles
1 mango, peeled and sliced
1 pineapple, peeled and cut into chunks
2 tangerines, peeled and sectioned
1 orange, peeled and sectioned
1 lime, cut into thin wedges

Instructions

1. Arrange the fruit on a tray with five sections, or artfully on a platter.
2. Put the lime wedges in a small bowl.

Diners can squeeze the lime over the fruit as they desire.

Serves 6–8.

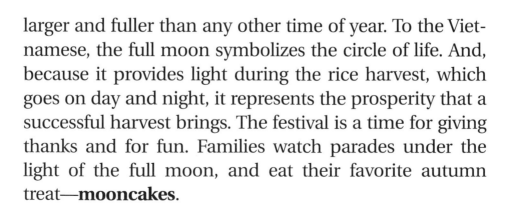

larger and fuller than any other time of year. To the Vietnamese, the full moon symbolizes the circle of life. And, because it provides light during the rice harvest, which goes on day and night, it represents the prosperity that a successful harvest brings. The festival is a time for giving thanks and for fun. Families watch parades under the light of the full moon, and eat their favorite autumn treat—**mooncakes**.

A Taste of the Moon

Mooncakes are flat, round, palm-sized pastries, similar to stuffed cookies. What makes them unique is their filling. Mooncakes are filled with a paste made from lotus seeds, a Vietnamese flowering water plant. The seeds are strung together like a long string of pearls, and dried in the sun. Then they are boiled, and ground

A cook rolls the rice flour dough (left) that he will use to make delicious mooncakes (below).

Mut

Eating candied fruits, nuts, seeds, roots, flowers, and vegetables is another Tet tradition. Before Tet, markets throughout Vietnam are a riot of color. Big glass jars filled with a huge assortment of dried, sugarcoated fruits, seeds, and vegetables known as mut are everywhere. There are candied rose petals, peach blossoms, apricots, kumquats, mandarin oranges, melon rinds, apples, carrots, squash, ginger, coconut, and watermelon and lotus seeds in a rainbow of colors. Some, like the watermelon seeds, are dyed a dazzling red, the color of good luck and happiness in Vietnam. Shoppers buy bags full of mut, which they arrange in colorful displays in their homes and serve to holiday guests.

Boxes of prepackaged mut line the shelves of a Vietnamese store during Tet.

into a sweet, moist paste. This process takes two to four weeks, which is why most people buy ready-made mooncakes from bakeries.

The paste, and an egg yolk are placed in the center of rich, sugary rice flour dough. The yolk forms a bright yellow moon inside each cake. Next, the mooncakes are put into a special mold that flattens them and imprints each one with a picture, such as a little moon. Finally the cakes are baked until they are moist and sweet. Author Linh Lam explains: "Everyone rushes to buy them before the festivities begin. Each cake is treasured."[16]

Whether sharing treasured mooncakes with family members, or eating chicken and banh chung at the holiday table, the Vietnamese love to gather together and celebrate. Special foods make every event more fun.

Metric Conversions

Mass (weight)

1 ounce (oz.)	= 28.0 grams (g)
8 ounces	= 227.0 grams
1 pound (lb.) or 16 ounces	= 0.45 kilograms (kg)
2.2 pounds	= 1.0 kilogram

Liquid Volume

1 teaspoon (tsp.)	= 5.0 milliliters (ml)
1 tablespoon (tbsp.)	= 15.0 milliliters
1 fluid ounce (oz.)	= 30.0 milliliters
1 cup (c.)	= 240 milliliters
1 pint (pt.)	= 480 milliliters
1 quart (qt.)	= 0.95 liters (l)
1 gallon (gal.)	= 3.80 liters

Pan Sizes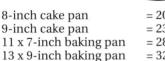

8-inch cake pan	= 20 x 4-centimeter cake pan
9-inch cake pan	= 23 x 3.5-centimeter cake pan
11 x 7-inch baking pan	= 28 x 18-centimeter baking pan
13 x 9-inch baking pan	= 32.5 x 23-centimeter baking pan
9 x 5-inch loaf pan	= 23 x 13-centimeter loaf pan
2-quart casserole	= 2-liter casserole

Temperature

212° F	= 100° C (boiling point of water)
225° F	= 110° C
250° F	= 120° C
275° F	= 135° C
300° F	= 150° C
325° F	= 160° C
350° F	= 180° C
375° F	= 190° C
400° F	= 200° C

Length

1/4 inch (in.)	= 0.6 centimeters (cm)
1/2 inch	= 1.25 centimeters
1 inch	= 2.5 centimeters

Chapter 1: Unique Ingredients

1. Diana My Tran, *The Vietnamese Cookbook*. Sterling, VA: Capitol, 2000, p. 14.
2. Quoted in Kate Heyhoe, "From Moon Cakes to Pancakes," *Kate's Global Kitchen*. www.globalgourmet. com/food/kgk/1099/kgk101699.html.
3. Corinne Trang, *Authentic Vietnamese Cooking*. New York: Simon & Schuster, 1999, p. 42.
4. Mai Pham, *Pleasures of the Vietnamese Table*. New York: HarperCollins, 2001, p. 41.

Chapter 2: A Delicious Mix

5. Quoted in R.W. Apple Jr. (Viet World Kitchen), "Looking Up an Old Love on the Streets of Vietnam," *New York Times*, August 13, 2003. www.vietworldkitchen.com/ bookshelf/articles/applenty.htm.
6. Tran, *The Vietnamese Cookbook*, p. 53.
7. Richard Sterling, *World Food Vietnam*. Victoria, Australia: Lonely Planet, 2000, p. 30.
8. Pham, *Pleasures of the Vietnamese Table*, p. 167.
9. Andrea Q. Nguyen (Viet World Kitchen), "Stalking the Sizzling Crepe," *Los Angeles Times*, February 9, 2005. www.vietworldkitchen.com/bookshelf/articles/ banhxeolat.htm.

Chapter 3: A Snack on Every Corner

10. Sterling, *World Food Vietnam*, p. 181.
11. Pham, *Pleasures of the Vietnamese Table*, p. 94.
12. Pham, *Pleasures of the Vietnamese Table*, p. 215.
13. Tran, *The Vietnamese Cookbook*, p. 110.

Chapter 4: Getting Together and Feasting

14. Trang, *Authentic Vietnamese Cooking*, p. 175.
15. Quoted in Mary Ann Eagle, "Tet Is Everybody's Birthday," Saveur.com, January/February 1998. www.saveur.com/article.jsp?ID=15438&typeID=100.
16. Linh Lam, "Tet Trung Thu and Mooncake Madness," Mamnon.org. www.mamnon.org/features/mooncake.html.

Glossary

baguettes: Thin, crunchy rolls.

banh: The Vietnamese word for any food item that can be eaten without chopsticks.

banh chung: A rice cake served during Tet.

che: Vietnamese pudding.

cilantro: Also known as coriander and Chinese parsley, this is a popular herb used in Vietnamese cooking.

claypot: A cooking pot made from clay and sand. It looks like a flowerpot with a lid.

coconut milk: The liquid squeezed from coconut meat.

crepes: Extremely thin pancakes.

garnishes: Toppings or trimmings that are added to food.

lemongrass: A grass used in Vietnamese cooking that gives food a lemony scent and flavor.

mooncakes: A stuffed cookie eaten during the Mid-Autumn Festival.

nuoc cham: A dipping sauce made from nuoc mam, garlic, water, sugar, hot peppers, and lime juice.

nuoc mam: A liquid drained from salted, fermented, anchovy-like fish used in Vietnamese cooking.

pâté: Finely ground or minced meat or chicken mixed with various spices.

pho: A popular noodle soup.

rice paper: Thin sheets made from rice flour and used as an edible food wrapping.

Tet: The Vietnamese New Year's holiday.

For Further Exploration

Books

Jennifer Ferro, *Vietnamese Foods & Culture.* Vero Beach, FL: Rourke, 1999. Looks at Vietnamese celebrations and the festive food that accompanies them.

Susan McKay, *Festivals of the World: Vietnam.* Milwaukee, WI: Gareth Stevens, 1997. Explores Tet and other Vietnamese holidays.

Peter Roop and Connie Roop, *A Visit to Vietnam.* Chicago: Heinemann Library, 1999. General information about Vietnam with maps and pictures.

Judith Simpson, *Ask About Asia—Vietnam.* Broomall, PA: Mason Crest, 2003. Explores the geography, history, and culture of Vietnam.

Susan Townsend, *World of Recipes: Vietnam.* Chicago: Heinemann Library, 2003. A Vietnamese cookbook for kids.

Web Sites

Adopt Vietnam (www.adoptvietnam.org). This Web site is for parents who adopt Vietnamese orphans and their children. It has information about Vietnamese holidays, recipes, Vietnamese art projects for kids, and maps of Vietnam.

American Museum of Natural History (www.amnh.org). Gives a virtual tour of a museum exhibit on Vietnam. Explores costumes, occupations, festivals, weddings, funerals, history, art, puppets, food, and markets with information, colored pictures, and numerous videos.

kidskonnect.com (www.kidskonnect.com/VietNam). A Web site for kids with lots of information about the Vietnam War, including a map.

Terragalleria (www.terragalleria.com/vietnam). A virtual art gallery featuring 700 different color photographs of Vietnam and the Vietnamese people.

Vietnamese Recipes and Cuisine (www.vietnamese-recipes.com). Provides over 1,000 recipes for Vietnamese dishes with articles and a glossary.

Index

Picture Credits

Cover Image: National Geographic/Getty Images
AFP/Getty Images, 45
Brand X Pictures/Getty Images, 23, 49, 50
© Catherine Karnow/CORBIS, 7, 21
Foodpix/Getty Images, 14, 38 (lower)
© Jeremy Horner/CORBIS, 19
© Kim T. Nguyen, 31, 32
© Leonard de Selva/CORBIS, 43
Lonely Planet Images, 24 (main and inset), 51 (main and inset)
© Nevada Wier/CORBIS, 52
© Owen Franken/CORBIS, 18, 27, 29, 37, 40
Photodisc Green/Getty Images, 11
PhotoDisc, 13, 20, 41
Photos.com, 38 (upper)
Robert Harding World Imagery/Getty Images, 15, 35
© Robert Maass/CORBIS, 22
© Robert van der Hilst/CORBIS, 8
© Steve Raymer/CORBIS, 9, 47
Stone/Getty Images, 33, 47 (inset)
Suzanne Santillan, 5
The Image Bank/Getty Images, 12

About the Author

Barbara Sheen has been an author and educator for more than 30 years. Her writing has been published in the United States and Europe. She lives in New Mexico with her family. In her spare time, she likes to swim, garden, walk, and bike. Of course, she loves to cook!